MW01226647

Up, Up, and Away!
Mandala Coloring Book

Hot Air Balloon Mandala Coloring Book.

by Patricia K Burian

www.pkburian.com

ISBN 13: 978-1546342830

ISBN 10: 1546342834

Welcome!

If you enjoy hot air balloons or ever dreamed of flying in one, here's your chance to ride high coloring your balloons. Make them bright as the sun or soft like floating on a cloud. Whatever you choose, have letting your creativity flow.

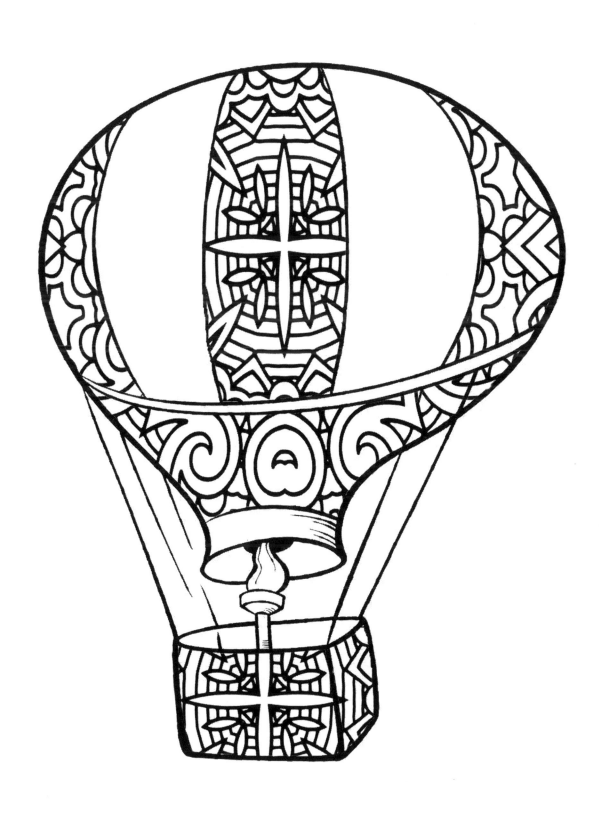

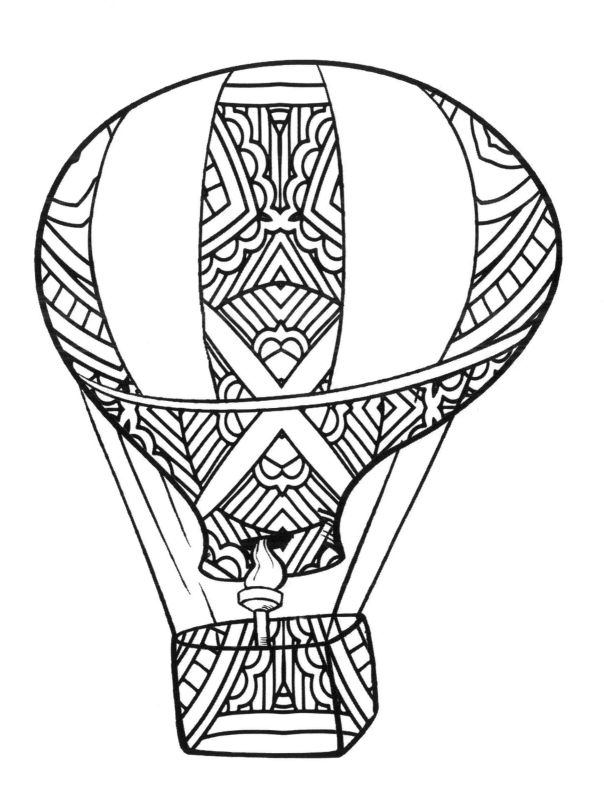

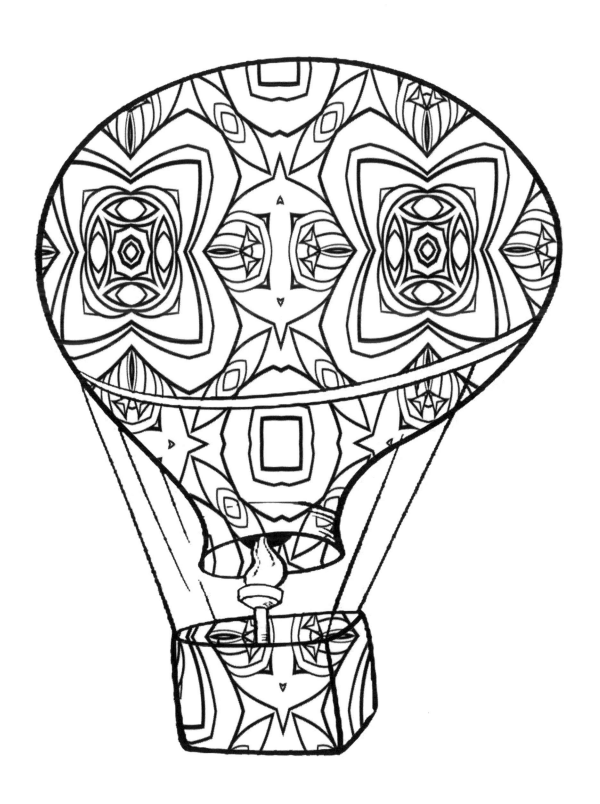

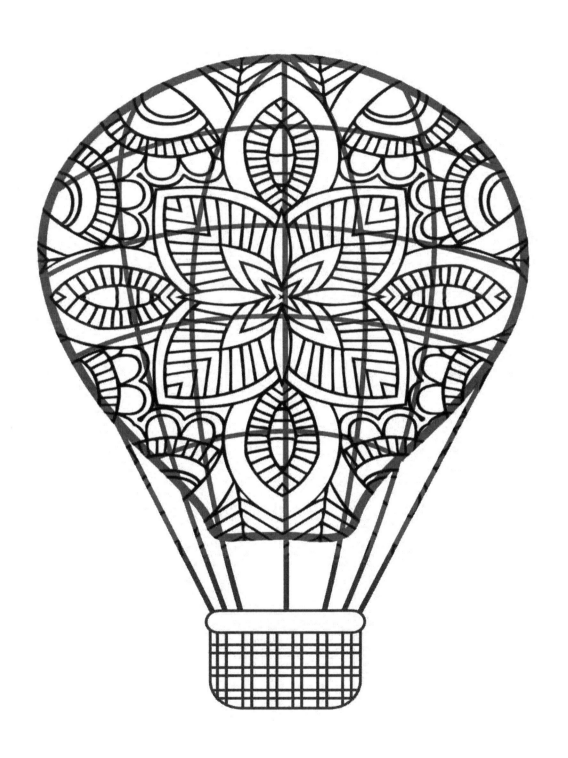

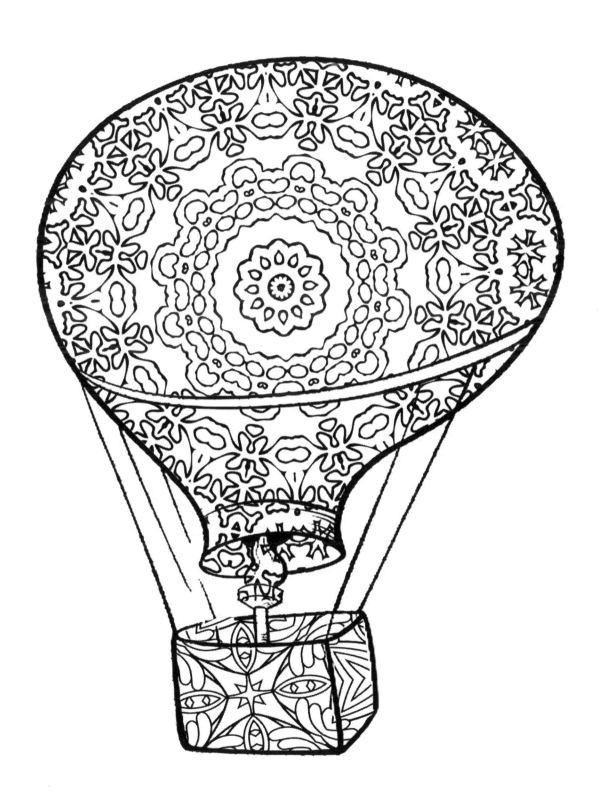

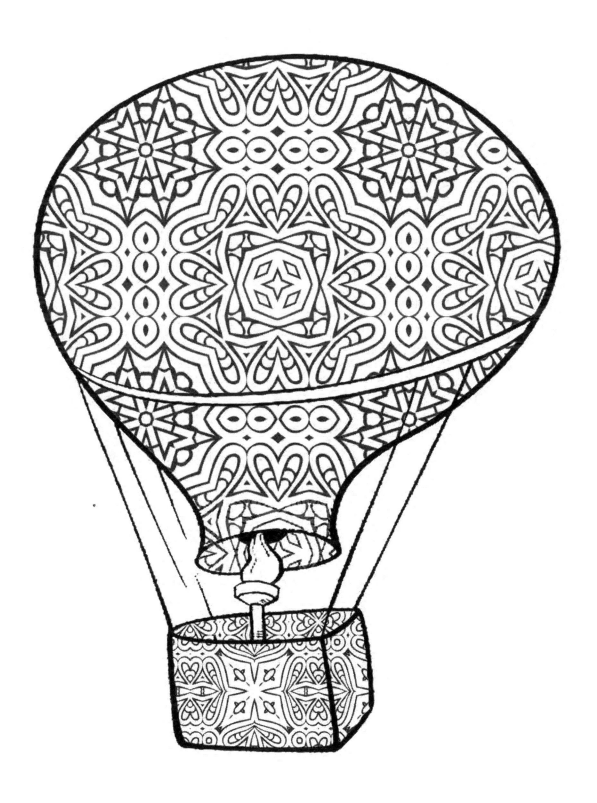

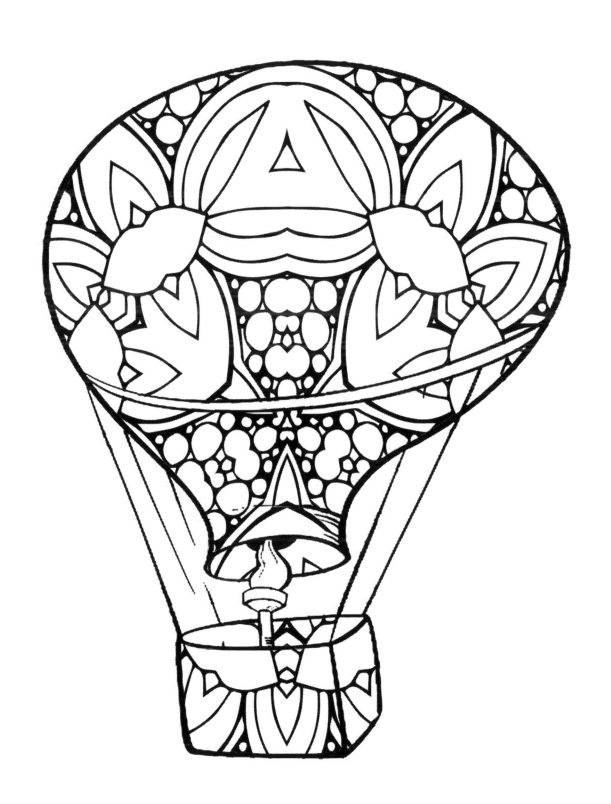

If you enjoyed coloring these hot air balloons, go to my web site to find more mandala coloring books at www.pkburian.com. Happy coloring!

Proof

Made in the USA
Columbia, SC
01 May 2017